A Season of Joy

Cherished Traditions and Heartwarming Moments

DR EMILY GREGORY

TABLE OF CONTENTS

INTRODUCTION

In a quaint village nestled amidst rolling hills, there lived a wise old storyteller named Samuel. Samuel was known far and wide for his ability to weave enchanting tales that captivated the hearts of both young and old. On a crisp autumn evening, as the golden leaves danced in the breeze, a group of eager children gathered around him, their eyes wide with anticipation.

With a twinkle in his eye, Samuel began to spin a tale of adventure and discovery. His words painted vivid images in the minds of his audience, transporting them to a world of magic and wonder. The children hung on every word, their imaginations ignited by the power of storytelling.

In that moment, it became evident that storytelling held a unique power—a power to inspire, educate, and connect people across generations. This ancient art form, passed down through centuries, continues to shape our lives and perspectives in ways we may not always realize.

In today's fast-paced world, where technology often dominates our attention, the timeless tradition of storytelling remains a beacon of light. It serves as a reminder of our shared humanity, allowing us to explore the depths of our emotions, the intricacies of our cultures, and the boundless possibilities of our imaginations.

As we embark on a journey through six inspirational storytelling ideas, let us remember the legacy of storytellers like Samuel, who have paved the way for us to discover the magic that lies within the tales we tell and hear. Together, we will unlock the potential to inspire, enlighten, and leave a lasting impact on those who lend us their ears.

CHAPTER ONE

Embracing the Gentle Arrival of Spring

As the world awakens from its winter slumber, there's a palpable shift in the air. The first whispers of spring breeze through, carrying with them the promise of renewal and the fragrance of blooming flowers. It's a time of gentle transition, a moment of grace as nature dons its vibrant hues once more. In this chapter, we embark on a journey through the tender embrace of spring, discovering the traditions that usher in this season of joy.

The Symphony of Nature

Picture this: a quiet morning, the air still crisp but tinged with warmth, birdsong filling the atmosphere with melodies of hope. This is the enchanting overture of spring. The world begins to unfurl, and everywhere you look, life is bursting forth in delicate buds and verdant shoots. It's a time of rebirth, a gentle reminder that even after the coldest of winters, there is an inevitable resurgence of life.

In these moments, take a pause. Step outside and let the caress of the spring breeze soothe your soul. Allow the sights and sounds of nature's awakening to wash over you. It's a symphony, a harmonious invitation to join in the dance of the seasons.

The Tradition of Blossoms and Baskets

Spring brings with it a cherished tradition that speaks to the heart of this season: the gathering of blossoms and the weaving of baskets. Imagine a leisurely stroll through a blossoming orchard, the soft petals of cherry blossoms falling around you like confetti. With each step, you gather these delicate treasures, creating a tapestry of color and fragrance.

Next comes the art of basket weaving. As the sun warms your back, you sit amidst nature's bounty, carefully intertwining slender reeds or flexible branches. The result is a vessel of beauty, ready to hold the essence of spring. These baskets become vessels of joy, carrying the spirit of the season into homes and hearts.

The Comfort of Spring Feasts

Spring is a time of feasting, of savoring the abundance that nature provides. Imagine a rustic table set beneath a blossoming tree, dappled sunlight casting a warm glow on the scene. The menu is simple yet exquisite - fresh greens, tender shoots, and the first fruits of the season. It's a celebration of nature's generosity, a reminder of the sustenance it offers.

Gather with loved ones, share stories, and revel in the flavors that spring bestows upon us. Let the taste of crisp asparagus and succulent strawberries linger on your palate, a reminder of the earth's bounty and the joy of coming together.

Finding Stillness in Spring

In the midst of the exuberance of spring, there lies a quiet sanctuary of stillness. It's in the moments when you find a secluded spot, perhaps beneath the embrace of a blossoming tree, and simply breathe. The world around you hums with life, but here, you are enveloped in a cocoon of tranquility.

Close your eyes and listen to the gentle rustle of leaves, the distant hum of bees, and the distant song of a thrush. Let the rhythm of nature lull you into a state of serene repose. In this stillness, you'll discover a profound connection to the season, a sense of belonging to the tapestry of life.

Embrace the Gentle Arrival

As we embrace the gentle arrival of spring, let us do so with open hearts and a deep sense of gratitude. This season offers us a chance to witness the miracle of rebirth, to participate in age-old traditions, and to find solace in moments of quiet reflection.

In the chapters that follow, we will continue this journey through the seasons, each one offering its own unique tapestry of traditions and moments of joy. But for now, let us revel in the tender embrace of spring, allowing it to weave its magic into our lives.

CHAPTER TWO

Basking in the Warmth of Summer's Embrace

As the days grow longer and the sun stretches its golden fingertips across the landscape, we find ourselves enveloped in the radiant embrace of summer. It's a season of vibrant vitality, of lazy afternoons and vibrant sunsets. In this chapter, we venture into the center of summer, uncovering the traditions that invite us to bask in its warm glow.

The Dance of Sunflowers

Picture this: a sun-drenched field, a sea of golden faces turned towards the heavens, their cheerful countenance mirroring the sun itself. This is the dance of sunflowers, a quintessential symbol of summer's exuberance. As you stroll amongst them, their towering presence becomes a source of both awe and comfort.

Gather a few of these bright blossoms, their golden crowns echoing the warmth of the sun. Place them in a vase, and immediately, your space is transformed into a sanctuary of summer. Let their cheerful disposition infuse your surroundings with a sense of pleasure and vitality.

The Symphony of Cicadas

As the day transitions into evening, a gentle hum permeates the air, rising and falling like the tide. It's the symphony of cicadas, a chorus that serenades the summer nights. Close your eyes and let their song flood over you. It's a lullaby, a reminder that even in the heat of summer, there is a rhythm of serenity and stillness.

Embrace this melody, let it lull you into a state of calm reverie. Allow the soothing hum to transport you away, a gentle reminder that even in the midst of life's fervor, there is a space for tranquility.

The Art of Fireflies and Lanterns

As twilight descends, the world takes on a mystical quality. Fireflies emerge from their concealing places, casting a soft, ethereal light upon the landscape. It's a ballet of light and shadow, a reminder of the enchantment that summer brings.

Gather with loved ones, each holding a lantern aglow with comforting light. Together, you'll embark on a voyage through the night, creating a path of luminescence.

It's a tradition that harkens back to simpler times, a ritual of togetherness and shared awe.

Savoring the Flavors of Summer

Summer's cornucopia is a treasure trove of flavors, a symphony of tastes that awaken the senses. Imagine the tangy sweetness of ripe apricots, the burst of juiciness from a freshly picked tomato, or the crisp crunch of a cucumber. These are the presents of summer's harvest.

Create a simple meal that gives homage to these seasonal delights. A salad of heirloom tomatoes drizzled with olive oil, a platter of grilled vegetables kissed by the flames, or a dish of succulent berries crowned with a dollop of cream. Let each mouthful be a celebration of the earth's generosity.

Dipping into Cool Waters

In the midst of summer's warmth, there is a yearning to seek refuge in the cool embrace of water. Whether it's a serene lake, a babbling brook, or the salty expanse of the ocean, these bodies of water beckon us to surrender to their soothing contact.

Take a moment to immerse yourself, to feel the soothing caress of water against your skin. Allow the coolness to cleanse away any tension, leaving you refreshed and rejuvenated. It's a simple act, yet one that conveys profound rejuvenation.

Embrace the Warmth of Summer's Embrace

As we immerse ourselves in the center of summer, let us do so with a spirit of openness and receptivity. This season offers us the gift of vibrant vitality, lazy afternoons, and moments of pure enchantment. In the chapters that follow, we will continue this voyage through the seasons, each one offering its own unique tapestry of traditions and moments of joy. But for now, let us revel in the warmth of summer's embrace, allowing it to infuse our lives with its radiant radiance.

CHAPTER THREE

Family Bond and Tradition: An Unbreakable Tapestry

In the heart of every cherished tradition lays the delicate thread of family bonds. These connections, woven through time, form an unbreakable tapestry that anchors us in the sea of life's changing tides. As we delve into this chapter, we embark on a journey through the moments that shape us, the traditions that define us, and the enduring love that binds us together.

The Hearth as Hearthstone

Imagine a hearth illuminated with the warmth of a crackling fire. Gathered around, generations gather together, their laughter and stories mingling in the air. Here, within the walls of home, rests the heartstone of family. It is a place where we are seen, heard, and cherished for who we are.

The hearth, both literal and metaphorical, contains the power to kindle not only physical warmth but also the fires of shared memories and aspirations.

In its glow, we find solace, fortitude, and a sense of belonging that transcends time.

Traditions: Threads of Continuity

As the seasons turn, so do the pages of our family's story. Through time-honored traditions, we bridge the divide between past and present, creating a seamless narrative of love and legacy. Picture a table set with familiar dishes, each recipe handed down through generations. With each shared meal, we partake in a communion of flavors and memories.

Whether it's the annual holiday gathering, a special ritual, or a simple bedtime story, traditions serve as touchstones, grounding us in the knowledge that we are part of something greater than ourselves. They give us origins, a sense of place in the grand tapestry of family history.

Tales from the Family Vault

Within the confines of photo albums, dusty journals, and cherished heirlooms, lies a treasure trove of stories begging to be told. These artifacts are more than mere relics; they are windows into the lives of those who came before us.

Through their eyes, we acquire a deeper understanding of our roots, our shared experiences, and the values that have guided us.

Unearth these tales, share them with younger generations, and let them serve as beacons of inspiration. In doing so, we honor the lives and legacies of those who came before us, ensuring that their stories carry on.

Celebrating Milestones: A Symphony of Shared Joy

Life is a journey characterized by milestones - births, graduations, weddings, and more. These moments of celebration provide opportunities to gather, to reaffirm our bonds, and to revel in the sheer pleasure of being together. Imagine a garden adorned with vibrant blooms, a testament to the beauty that emerges when we join together in love and celebration.

In these moments, we create memories that will be etched in our hearts eternally. They serve as anchors in the passage of time, reminding us that no matter where life takes us, we are eternally connected by the shared joy of these milestones.

Nurturing the Flame: Passing Down Values and Traditions

As custodians of family legacy, it falls to us to impart the values and traditions that have defined us. Through open conversations, shared experiences, and acts of compassion, we pass down the torch of wisdom, love, and resilience.

Picture an elder imparting life lessons to a wide-eyed youngster, their features bathed in the soft glow of twilight. It is in these moments of mentorship and guidance that we forge a bridge between the past and the future, ensuring that the flame of our family's legacy continues to burn vividly.

Embracing Our Shared Story

In the depths of family bonds and cherished traditions, we find a sanctuary of love, acceptance, and belonging. This chapter is an homage to the tapestry of family, woven with threads of shared history and enduring affection. As we navigate the pages that follow, let us do so with a heart full of gratitude for the ties that bind us, and a profound appreciation for the traditions that shape our lives.

CHAPTER FOUR

Festive Feasts and Culinary Delights: Nourishing Body and Soul

Welcome to a chapter that awakens the senses and invites you to embark on a journey through the delectable world of festive feasts and culinary delights. Picture a table adorned with an array of dishes, their aromas mingling in the air, promising a symphony of flavors to tantalize your taste buds. In this chapter, we celebrate the art of nourishment, not just for the body, but for the soul as well.

The Dance of Flavors

Food is more than sustenance; it is an expression of love, creativity, and cultural heritage. Imagine the sizzle of a hot pan, the gentle simmering of a fragrant stew, and the rhythmic chopping of fresh herbs. These are the sounds of a culinary dance, where ingredients come together to create a harmonious symphony of flavors.

Each dish tells a story, carrying with it the essence of tradition and the spirit of celebration. Whether it's a cherished family recipe or a newfound culinary adventure, every bite is an opportunity to savor the rich tapestry of flavors that life has to offer.

From Garden to Table: A Celebration of Freshness

There's a special magic in growing your own produce, nurturing it from seed to harvest, and then transforming it into a culinary masterpiece. Picture a sun-kissed garden, vibrant with colors and fragrances. Here, we find a connection to the earth, a reminder of the beauty and abundance that nature provides.

In this chapter, we explore the joy of sourcing ingredients from our own gardens or local markets, celebrating the seasons and the bounties they bring. From crisp salads to hearty stews, the freshness of the ingredients elevates every dish to a new level of sensory delight.

The Art of Hosting: Creating Memorable Dining Experiences

Setting a table is akin to creating a canvas for a work of art. Each element - from the choice of tableware to the arrangement of flowers - contributes to the overall experience. Imagine a beautifully laid table, bathed in soft candlelight, inviting guests to gather and share in the joy of a carefully curated meal.

In this chapter, we delve into the nuances of hosting, offering tips on how to create a welcoming atmosphere that encourages connection and conversation. Whether it's an intimate dinner for two or a festive gathering of many, the art of hosting is about creating moments that linger in the hearts of your guests.

Culinary Traditions: A Taste of Heritage

Every culture has its own culinary treasures, passed down through generations like precious heirlooms. These recipes are more than just a combination of ingredients; they are a living testament to the traditions that define us. Picture a kitchen filled with the comforting aroma of dishes that have been lovingly prepared for decades.

In this chapter, we celebrate the richness of culinary heritage, exploring recipes that have stood the test of time. From the spicy aromas of Indian curry to the comforting embrace of Italian pasta, these dishes connect us to our roots and remind us of the shared history that unites us.

The Joy of Shared Meals

There is a unique magic that happens when we gather around a table to share a meal. It is a time of connection, of laughter, and of the simple joy of being together. Imagine the warmth that fills the room as loved ones come together to break bread and share stories.

In this chapter, we delve into the significance of shared meals, offering insights into how they strengthen bonds and create lasting memories. Whether it's a Sunday brunch with family or a potluck dinner with friends, the act of coming together around a table is a celebration of love and togetherness.

A Feast for the Senses

As we navigate the culinary landscape of this chapter, may you be inspired to embrace the joy of preparing and sharing meals with loved ones. Let the flavors, aromas, and textures ignite your senses, and may every meal be a celebration of life's abundant blessings.

CHAPTER FIVE

Milestones and Memorable Moments: Celebrating Life's Journeys

Welcome to a chapter that invites you to pause, reflect, and revel in the beauty of life's milestones and memorable moments. This is a sanctuary of cherished recollections, a space where we honor the journeys we've undertaken and the moments that have left an indelible mark on our hearts.

Embracing Milestones: Markers of Growth and Achievement

Life is a tapestry woven with threads of achievements, both big and small. Picture a quilt, each patch representing a milestone reached, a goal accomplished. In this chapter, we take a moment to acknowledge and celebrate these significant markers of growth.

From graduations to promotions, from the birth of a child to the completion of a personal project, milestones are the stepping stones that pave our paths forward. They are a testament to our resilience, our determination, and our capacity for growth.

Capturing Memories: The Power of Photographs and Keepsakes

In the digital age, photographs have become our visual time capsules, preserving moments that would otherwise slip through the sands of time. Imagine flipping through an album, each image a portal to a specific moment in the past. In this chapter, we delve into the art of capturing memories.

From the click of a camera to the artful arrangement of mementos, we explore the various ways in which we can immortalize the moments that matter most. These visual keepsakes serve as touchstones, grounding us in the beauty of the present while offering glimpses into the tapestry of our past.

Commemorative Rituals: Honoring Special Occasions

Rituals are the threads that bind us to our cultural heritage, providing a sense of continuity and belonging. Picture a family gathered around a table, passing down stories and traditions from one generation to the next. In this chapter, we delve into the significance of commemorative rituals.

Whether it's a birthday celebration, a religious ceremony, or a cultural festival, these rituals serve as anchors, reminding us of our roots and the values that define us. They are a source of comfort, a reminder that we are part of something larger than ourselves.

Reflection and Gratitude: Finding Meaning in the Moments

In the hustle and bustle of daily life, it's easy to overlook the significance of the moments that shape our journeys. Imagine taking a moment to sit in quiet reflection, to let the experiences of the past wash over you. In this chapter, we explore the power of reflection and gratitude.

By pausing to acknowledge the beauty and complexity of our journeys, we find meaning in the tapestry of our lives. Gratitude becomes our compass, guiding us towards a deeper appreciation for the moments, both ordinary and extraordinary, that have shaped us.

A Tapestry of Stories: Sharing Narratives of Triumph and Resilience

Every milestone is a story waiting to be told, a narrative of triumph over adversity, of growth in the face of challenges. Picture a gathering of loved ones, each one sharing their own tales of resilience and accomplishment. In this chapter, we celebrate the power of storytelling.

Through the sharing of our journeys, we find connection and inspiration. We realize that we are not alone in our experiences, that our stories are woven into the larger fabric of human existence. These narratives serve as beacons of hope, reminding us of the strength that resides within us.

Celebrating the Journey

As we navigate this chapter, may you find solace in the celebration of life's milestones and memorable moments. May you be inspired to cherish the journey, to honor the past, and to embrace the future with open arms. In every milestone, in every memory, may you discover the profound beauty of a life well-lived.

CHAPTER SIX

Seasonal Reflections and Gratitude: Embracing the Rhythms of Nature

In this chapter, we step into the gentle ebb and flow of the seasons, finding solace in their cyclical dance. It is a time to pause, to breathe in the crisp air of autumn, to feel the warmth of summer's embrace, and to witness the rebirth of spring. Here, we explore the art of seasonal reflections and the transformative power of gratitude.

The Symphony of Seasons: Nature's Ever-changing Canvas

Nature, with its ever-changing hues and melodies, offers us a profound tapestry of inspiration. Imagine a canvas painted with the vibrant reds of autumn leaves, the soft blanket of snow in winter, the burst of colors in a spring meadow, and the golden kiss of summer's sun. In this section, we delve into the symphony of seasons.

Each season carries its own unique energy, inviting us to align with the rhythms of nature. As the leaves fall and the world prepares for winter's slumber, we too can turn inward, reflecting on the chapters of our lives.

With the arrival of spring, we find renewal and the promise of new beginnings. Summer calls us to bask in the fullness of life, while autumn whispers of transition and letting go.

The Art of Seasonal Rituals: Nurturing the Soul

Rituals provide us with an anchor amidst the ever-changing tides of life. Picture a quiet winter evening, where the soft glow of candles illuminates a room, or a summer gathering beneath a canopy of stars. In this section, we explore the art of crafting seasonal rituals.

Whether it's a solstice celebration, a winter meditation, or a summer picnic, these rituals serve as touchstones, grounding us in the present moment. They offer a sense of continuity, connecting us to the traditions of our ancestors and the natural world. Through these rituals, we find a deeper sense of belonging and a renewed appreciation for the beauty that surrounds us.

Cultivating Gratitude: Nourishing the Heart

Gratitude is the gentle undercurrent that flows through the tapestry of our lives, weaving moments of joy and contentment into the fabric of our existence.

Imagine the warmth that spreads through your heart when you take a moment to appreciate the simple pleasures of a summer breeze or the cozy embrace of a winter blanket. In this section, we delve into the transformative power of gratitude.

By cultivating gratitude, we open ourselves to the abundance that surrounds us. We learn to see beauty in the small details, to find joy in everyday moments. Gratitude becomes a companion on our journey, guiding us towards a deeper sense of fulfillment and contentment.

Embracing the Seasons, Embracing Ourselves

As we navigate this chapter, may you find comfort in the rhythm of the seasons, in the beauty of nature's ever-changing canvas. May you be inspired to craft meaningful rituals that nurture your soul, and may you cultivate gratitude as a source of sustenance for your heart. In the embrace of the seasons, may you discover a profound sense of belonging and a deeper connection to the world around you.

Chapter SEVEN

Spreading Joy to Others: Nurturing Hearts, Creating Smiles

Welcome to a chapter that celebrates the beautiful art of giving and the boundless pleasure it brings. In "Spreading Joy to Others," we investigate the profound impact of kindness and the transformative power of thoughtful gestures. It is a voyage of nurturing hearts and creating smiles, a reminder that even the smallest acts of generosity can illuminate the world.

The Ripple Effect of Kindness: Illuminating Lives

Kindness is a radiant force that knows no bounds. It is a language understood by all, a universal currency of love and compassion. When we extend our hand in kindness, we set off a ripple effect that affects lives in ways we may never fully comprehend.

Imagine a world where every act of kindness, no matter how modest, reverberates through the hearts of many. It is in this realm of shared humanity that we find the true essence of giving.

Through compassionate gestures, we become beacons of light, igniting hope and warmth in the lives of others.

Thoughtful Tokens: Gifts from the Heart Gift-giving is an exquisite ballet of love and appreciation. It is a tangible expression of our feelings, a means to say, "You matter, and you are cherished." In this section, we embark on a journey through the discipline of thoughtful giving.

A meticulously selected gift speaks volumes. It tells a story of the recipient's uniqueness, a testament to the profundity of our connection. It need not be extravagant; it is the thought, the sentiment behind it, that contains the true magic. Whether a handcrafted token or a cherished keepsake, each gift becomes a vessel of love, conveying with it the warmth of our intentions.

The Present of Presence: A Gift Beyond Measure

In a world that often rushes ahead, the gift of presence stands as a sanctuary of solace. Picture a moment of shared silence, of being completely present with a loved one. It is in these instances that true connection flourishes, where hearts speak a language only they understand.

Being present for others is a gift that requires no wrapping, no ribbons. It is the straightforward act of showing up, of listening with intent, of being there in both body and spirit. It tells those we care about that they are valued, that their presence in our lives is a cherished blessing.

Embracing the Joy of Giving

As we traverse through this chapter, may you find inspiration in the pleasure of giving. May you recognize the profound impact of your kindness, no matter how minor it may seem. Know that each gesture, each gift, each instant of presence, contributes to a brighter, more compassionate world.

In the act of spreading joy to others, we discover a sense of purpose that transcends our individual lives. We become threads in the tapestry of humanity, weaving together moments of shared kindness and affection. Remember, in giving, we receive in abundance, for the truest pleasure lies in nurturing the hearts of others and creating smiles that light up the world.

CHAPTER EIGHT

Navigating Challenges with Grace: Finding Strength in Adversity

In the journey of life, obstacles are the threads that add depth and texture to our experiences. They test our resilience, prompting us to seek the wellspring of power within. "Navigating Challenges with Grace" invites you to embark on a journey through adversity, giving insights and tools to face life's trials with courage and composure.

Embracing the Ebb and Flow: Understanding Life's Natural Rhythm

Life, much like the water, has its ebbs and flows. There are moments of calm peace and times of turbulent waves. Understanding this natural rhythm helps us to handle challenges with a steadied heart. It reminds us that adversity is not a deviation from the road but an integral part of the journey.

Through the lens of grace, we learn to accept both the peaks and dips of life. We find solace in the knowledge that every challenge is a stepping stone, taking us to greater self-discovery and wisdom.

In this part, we delve into the art of embracing life's ebb and flow, finding solace in the impermanence of all things.

Cultivating Inner Resilience: The Power Within Resilience is the cornerstone of navigating obstacles with grace. It is the inner fortitude that allows us to bend without breaking, to weather storms and emerge better on the other side. Cultivating this inner resilience is a gift we give to ourselves, a refuge of strength that stands unyielding.

In this chapter, we study practices and perspectives that nurture our resilience. From mindfulness to self-compassion, from finding support to tapping into our innate wisdom, we uncover the tools that empower us to face adversity with grace. Together, we learn that within each of us lies a wellspring of power waiting to be tapped.

The Dance of Acceptance: Finding Peace in What Is

Acceptance is the gentle surrender to what is, a dance with life's ever-changing scenery. It is not resignation, but a conscious choice to make peace with the present time. Through acceptance, we free ourselves from the shackles of resistance, allowing us to move forward with grace and calm.

In this part, we delve into the art of acceptance, giving practices and insights to embrace life's challenges with an open heart. We learn that in acceptance, we find liberation, a sense of lightness that accompanies the release of resistance. It is a powerful tool that transforms our interaction with adversity.

Navigating Challenges with Grace: A Transformative Journey

As we journey through this chapter, may you find solace in the knowledge that challenges are not roadblocks, but chances for growth. May you find the wellspring of strength that lies within, ready to rise up and meet any adversity with grace and composure.

Remember, it is in the crucible of difficulties that we forge the steel of our character. Each trial is a teacher, each failure a stepping stone. With grace as our guide, we manage the intricate dance of life, weaving threads of strength, wisdom, and resilience.

In "Navigating Challenges with Grace," you are invited to start on a transformative journey, to embrace the ebb and flow of life, to develop inner resilience, and to dance with acceptance. Through these practices, may you find not only the strength to face obstacles, but the grace to do so with an open heart and a steady spirit.

Chapter NINE

Savoring the Present, Anticipating the Future: Embracing the Joys of Now and Tomorrow

In the hustle and bustle of life, it's easy to get caught up in the whirlwind of responsibilities and plans. Yet, amidst the flurry of activity, there lies a treasure trove of moments waiting to be savored. "Savoring the Present, Anticipating the Future" invites you to slow down, to relish the beauty of the present, and to look ahead with hopeful anticipation.

Embracing the Gift of Now: Finding Joy in the Present Moment

The present moment is a gift, a precious jewel waiting to be uncovered. It holds the whispers of nature, the warmth of a loved one's smile, and the simple pleasures that often go unnoticed. In this section, we embark on a journey to embrace the richness of now.

Through mindfulness and presence, we learn to fully engage with each moment, allowing it to unfold with grace. We discover that in the stillness of now, there is a profound sense of contentment and joy.

It is a practice that invites us to be fully alive, to drink deeply from the wellspring of the present.

Cultivating Hope and Vision: Anticipating a Bright Tomorrow

Anticipation is the spark that ignites our dreams, the compass that guides us towards the future. It is the gentle whisper that reminds us that there are chapters yet unwritten, adventures yet to be embarked upon. In this chapter, we explore the art of anticipating the future with hope and vision.

Through introspection and intention, we tap into our inner well of creativity and possibility. We set forth our aspirations, painting a vivid picture of the tomorrows we yearn for. Together, we learn that anticipation is not just a yearning for what's to come, but an active participation in shaping our destiny.

Balancing the Dance: Weaving the Threads of Now and Tomorrow

Savoring the present and anticipating the future are not opposing forces, but harmonious partners in the dance of life. In this section, we delve into the art of finding equilibrium between the two.

We learn that by grounding ourselves in the present, we gain the clarity and strength to move towards the future.

Through practices that nurture both presence and vision, we become adept at balancing the demands of today with the aspirations of tomorrow. It is a delicate interplay, a dance of grace and intention. Together, we discover that in this balance lies a sense of purpose and fulfillment that permeates every facet of our lives.

Savoring the Present, Anticipating the Future: A Tapestry of Joy and Hope

As we journey through this chapter, may you find solace in the knowledge that the present and the future are not separate realms, but interconnected threads in the tapestry of life. May you relish each moment as a precious gem, and may you step forward with hope and vision towards the horizon of your dreams.

Remember, it is in the delicate dance between savoring the present and anticipating the future that we find true fulfillment. Each moment holds the potential for wonder, and each tomorrow is a canvas waiting for your brushstrokes. With an open heart and a hopeful spirit, may you navigate this dance with grace and joy.

CHAPTER TEN

A Legacy of Joy: Nurturing Happiness for Generations to Come

As we journey through life, we are bestowed with the profound opportunity to leave behind a legacy—a legacy of love, kindness, and above all, joy. "A Legacy of Joy" invites you to reflect on the beautiful tapestry of moments you have woven throughout your life and to consider how you can pass on the torch of happiness to future generations.

Embracing the Power of Intergenerational Joy

In the heart of every family lies the potential to create a chain reaction of joy that spans generations. In this section, we explore the power of intergenerational connections. We delve into the traditions, stories, and experiences that bind us together, creating a tapestry of shared joy.

Through the passing down of cherished traditions and the sharing of heartwarming stories, we create a bridge that links the past, the present, and the future. We learn that our actions today have the power to shape the happiness of those who come after us.

Nurturing Resilience and Strength: Building Foundations for Joyful Tomorrows

A legacy of joy is not built solely on fleeting moments of happiness, but on the enduring pillars of resilience and strength. In this chapter, we explore how to instill these qualities in the hearts of our loved ones, ensuring that they have the tools to navigate life's journey with grace.

Through the sharing of wisdom gained from our own experiences, we offer guidance and support to those who will follow in our footsteps. We become beacons of light, illuminating the path towards a joyful and purposeful life.

Passing Down the Torch: Cultivating a Culture of Happiness

The true essence of a legacy lies not in possessions or accolades, but in the intangible gifts of love, laughter, and happiness. In this section, we delve into practical ways to cultivate a culture of joy within our families and communities.

By leading with kindness, by demonstrating the power of gratitude, and by fostering an environment of acceptance and love, we lay the foundation for a legacy that will continue to flourish for generations to come. Together, we discover that the seeds of joy we plant today have the potential to blossom into a garden of happiness for the future.

A Legacy of Joy: Your Gift to the World

As we reflect on the tapestry of moments that make up our lives, let us remember that our legacy is not measured by the wealth we accumulate, but by the joy we sow. May this chapter serve as a gentle reminder that you have the power to leave behind a legacy of immeasurable value—a legacy of joy.

With each act of kindness, with each shared laugh, and with each moment of genuine connection, you are contributing to a legacy that will touch hearts for generations to come. As you embark on this journey of creating a legacy of joy, may you do so with a heart full of love and a spirit brimming with hope.

CONCLUSION

As we come to the end of this heartfelt journey through "A Season of Joy: Cherished Traditions and Heartwarming Moments," it is with a profound sense of gratitude and fulfillment that we reflect on the tapestry of experiences we have woven together. This book has been a celebration of the moments that bring warmth to our hearts, the traditions that bind us together, and the legacy of joy that we have the privilege to pass on.

Throughout the chapters, we have explored the significance of meaningful connections in our lives. From the embrace of family bonds to the camaraderie of shared experiences, we have witnessed the transformative power of genuine human connection. It is within these connections that we find the true essence of joy—a sense of belonging, acceptance, and unconditional love.

Gratitude has been a cornerstone of our journey. We have learned that in every moment, no matter how ordinary or extraordinary, there is a gift waiting to be acknowledged. Through the practice of gratitude, we open our hearts to the abundance that surrounds us.

We come to understand that joy is not solely found in grand gestures, but in the simple, everyday blessings that grace our lives.

As we bid farewell to these pages, let us carry forward the lessons and insights that have touched our hearts. Let us continue to cherish our traditions, to embrace our loved ones, and to spread the light of joy to those we encounter on our journey. May we be beacons of kindness, radiating warmth and love into the world.

In the end, it is not the material possessions we leave behind, but the imprint of joy we leave on the hearts of others. As we step into each new day, may we do so with open hearts and a commitment to live a life filled with the boundless joy that this season has bestowed upon us. This is our legacy of joy, our gift to the world.